FRIAR JACK'S FAVORITE PRAYERS

| | |

OTHER BOOKS BY FRIAR JACK WINTZ

St. Francis in San Francisco

A Retreat with Pope John Paul II: Be Not Afraid

Anthony of Padua: Saint of the People

Will I See My Dog in Heaven?

I Will See You in Heaven

Friar Jack's
favorite prayers

Jack Wintz, O.F.M.

ST. ANTHONY MESSENGER PRESS
Cincinnati, Ohio

| | |

For all my coworkers at
St. Anthony Messenger Press

Cover and book design by Mark Sullivan
Cover photo by Frank Jasper, O.F.M.

LIBRARY OF CONGRESS CATALOGING-IN-PUBLICATION DATA
Wintz, Jack.
Friar Jack's favorite prayers / Jack Wintz.
p. cm.
ISBN 978-0-86716-991-1 (acid-free paper)
1. Catholic Church—Prayers and devotions. I. Title.
BX2149.2.W58 2011
242'.802—dc22
2010047951

ISBN 978-0-86716-991-1
Copyright ©2011, Jack Wintz. All rights reserved.
Published by St. Anthony Messenger Press
28 W. Liberty St.
Cincinnati, OH 45202
www.AmericanCatholic.org
www.SAMPBooks.org

Printed in the United States of America.
Printed on acid-free paper.

11 12 13 14 15 5 4 3 2 1

| | |

C O N T E N T S

INTRODUCTION: Pathways of Prayer   { x }

CHAPTER ONE: The Apostles' Creed   { 1 }

CHAPTER TWO: The Glory Be   { 9 }

CHAPTER THREE: The Our Father   { 15 }

CHAPTER FOUR: *Anima Christi*   { 23 }

CHAPTER FIVE: Come, Holy Spirit   { 33 }

CHAPTER SIX: The Magnificat   { 41 }

CHAPTER SEVEN: The Hail Mary   { 49 }

CHAPTER EIGHT: The Canticle of the Creatures   { 55 }

CHAPTER NINE: St. Francis' Prayer Before the Crucifix   { 61 }

CHAPTER TEN: The Franciscan Coat of Arms   { 71 }

CHAPTER ELEVEN: The Way of the Cross   { 75 }

CHAPTER TWELVE: I See His Blood Upon the Rose   { 83 }

CHAPTER THIRTEEN: St. Anthony and the Child Jesus   { 89 }

CHAPTER FOURTEEN: The Peace Prayer of St. Francis   { 97 }

CHAPTER FIFTEEN: A Prayer of St. Clare   { 107 }

NOTES   { 112 }

Pathways of Prayer

Before I happily share with you my favorite prayers and reflections, I want to offer you an overview of some methods or styles of prayer that many people who love to pray find themselves using. So let me start with a few personal thoughts about prayer.

As I look at it, to pray is to communicate with God. I like to compare prayer to a radio that is not properly tuned into a station. The news reporters or entertainers are out there talking or singing away. But if I have not turned on the radio or tuned into the station correctly, there can be no communication. This is often our problem with God. God is out there—as well as inside us—beaming forth love, goodness, and inspiration, but it's lost on us because we fail to tune in properly or open ourselves properly to God's loving presence.

Actually, there are many prayer-paths to God available to us today. As a Franciscan friar and writer, I have collected many ideas for enriching a life of prayer. They come from books and articles, from interviews with spiritual advisors, and from my own prayer experience. In this introduction, I will discuss several methods or pathways of prayer by which the Spirit can lead us into living union with God.

Recognizing What You Already Have

Whether we know it or not, we are already in the presence of God and united with God because God is everywhere. Prayer helps us bring to consciousness the precious bond we have with God and God's saving love. As twentieth-century Trappist monk and spiritual writer Thomas Merton points out: "In prayer we discover what we already have.... We already have everything, but we don't know it and we don't experience what we already possess.... The whole thing boils down to giving ourselves in prayer a chance to realize that we have what we seek. We don't have to rush after it. It is there all the time and, if we give it time, it will make itself known to us."[1]

Like grace, of course, God's presence is a gift, and we cannot force ourselves into a living communion with God by a sheer act of will. Human friendship is similar. We cannot force another man or woman to be our friend or lover. We can only offer our friendship to another and then humbly await the gift of his or her friendship. The essence of prayer consists in this humble waiting—in a childlike spirit of openness, expectation, and listening. To pray means to make ourselves present and available to God so that we are truly ready to open the door when Jesus comes and knocks.

Each of us is wise to find the styles of prayer that suit us. The Holy Spirit is the only true teacher of prayer, and without preconceived ideas, we must let the Spirit draw us to those ways of prayer that work best for us. If any of the following suggestions are helpful for you, wonderful. If any seem out of sync with your temperament or cause you anxiety, steer clear of them. Any good spiritual director will warn you against methods of prayer that do not harmonize with your spiritual gifts. With this in mind, feel free to explore the following pathways or approaches to prayer:

Familiar Prayers

Come, Holy Spirit, the Our Father, the Stations of the Cross, and the Peace Prayer of St. Francis are but a few samples of Christianity's rich tradition of prayer. And when slowly pondered, the sentiments and phrases of the Our Father or Come, Holy Spirit, for example, have great potential as passageways into the presence of God.

And let's not overlook the Eucharist as Christianity's most perfect prayer and primary pathway leading us as a body of believers—and as individuals—into union with God.

Prayers of Praise

Praise is a form of prayer that belongs near the top of anyone's list. Joyful and free, it preserves us from the false notion that prayer is cheerless. Praise is the bubbling over of the Spirit. Often the Spirit's first impulse within us is that of bursting into praise and thanksgiving. Surely, one of our deepest human instincts is adoration, and we do well to let the Spirit flow freely through us in words of praise. The Our Father recognizes this in its first exclamation: "Hallowed by thy name!"

Praise and adoration take us from our self-preoccupation and lead us outward to God and to the creation that bears God's imprint. This is the key to the prayer of St. Francis of Assisi, according to Franciscan author Murray Bodo. Like St. Francis, the Spirit prompts us to celebrate our brotherhood and sisterhood with other creatures and praise God, not in isolation from creation, but through sunlight, rain, wind, and flowers. It's always a good time for you and me to spend some time praising God in an outdoor park or garden on at the lake or seacoast.

Prayer of Inner Quiet

One of the richest forms of prayer occurs when the heart is absolutely quiet. As the psalmist says, "Be still, and know that I am God..." (Psalm 46:10). Several years ago, Dominican Sister Sylvia Rosell from the Still Point House of Prayer of Albany, New York, explained it to me this way:

> If you still your mind, you can hear your own heart. And at the core of your heart is the indwelling of God. It's just like when you love someone and you sit there and look at each other. You just stare silently and there is a terrible presence between you. It's an awesome thing. God is present and you are present—to each other. It's a matter of just being there.[2]

Fr. William Johnston, S.J., the author of several books on prayer, also commented on this prayer of inner quiet or silent union with God. The natural drift of prayer, Johnston says, is often *from words to silence*. At times we feel led, as if by a hidden inner compass, into this kind of silent union with God.

At other times, however, the best form of prayers for us may be prayers that rely on words. In fact, Fr. Johnston cautions against striving too hard to get rid of words and thoughts. Yet, he believes we should be conscious of those times the Spirit is moving us to silence. "It's like there are two layers of the psyche," he explains. "In one layer there are lots of words and thoughts going on, but on a deeper level, you are united quietly to God." When you feel drawn to silent union, go there and rest in God as long as the Spirit invites.[3]

Prayer of Listening
This is really another aspect of the prayer of inner quiet, but the focus is on *listening to God* who reveals himself in our inmost being. In this prayer you listen at the very core of your being to the deepest voice of all—the voice of God and of the Spirit. Thomas Merton describes this kind of prayer as "finding one's deepest center, awakening the profound depths of our being in the presence of God, who is the source of our being and our life."[4]

A Prayer of Silent Union with God
You may find it helpful to do this form of prayer that I was inspired to compose some years ago on the basis of ideas presented above:

> Just sit down and, keeping your back straight but free, begin quieting your mind and your body by taking a few relaxing breaths. Center your awareness on the silent and infinite presence of God within your heart.
>
> Let the Spirit lead you beyond the noisy world of space and time into the silent realm within you where God dwells as the source and ground of your being. Center your attention on that hushed point within you where the human touches the divine, where (you) the branch intersects with the Vine—where you and God are one and dwell in each other. Let yourself sink into

the silent immensity of God. Simply let your praying become a silent being there with God. Without any need for thoughts and words, exchange quiet love with God for as long as you feel inspired.

Prayer of Petition

Prayers of petition, otherwise known as prayers of intercession or of asking God for personal favors, have sometimes been downplayed in recent years, because, to some observers, such prayers may seem self-centered and immature. This could be especially true in the case where one prays to win a football game or pass a test for which one did not study. If our prayer is too self-centered or mundane, certainly we may want to broaden our horizons or turn more to prayers of praise and of loving union with God.

On the other hand, to see intercessory prayer as immature or below our dignity is to fail to recognize our true status as finite creatures. Even in human love, those who are too proud or pure to receive love from another person and only see themselves as givers do not make the best lovers. As Thomas Merton writes in *No Man Is an Island*, "The man whose prayer is so pure that he never asks God for anything does not know who God is, and does not know himself, for he does not know his own need for God."[5] Like Christ himself, we should not hesitate to recognize our dependence on God and pray for our daily needs and, of course, those of our neighbor.

Prayer of Suffering

Those of us suffering pain, heartbreak, or loss can turn even these experiences into prayer, according to Fr. Johnston. We strive to remain with God and with Jesus, our healer, instead of trying to escape the pain or the void or to seek consolation right away from others.

Fr. Johnston suggests that "you don't run away [from pain]. You stay with it. You stay in the void because that can open up to God and real joy. If you remain with God and with the pain, a new understanding can come to the whole thing. The void may open up to God within." Jesus is our model for the prayer of suffering. In the Garden of Gethsemane, he was racked with pain and fear. Though it was not easy, Jesus lovingly opened himself the more to trust and vital contact with his loving Father.

In the following pages, I am happy to share with you some of my favorite prayers and reflections.

The Apostles' Creed

I believe in God, the Father Almighty,
Creator of heaven and earth;
and in Jesus Christ, his only Son, our Lord.
who was conceived by the Holy Spirit,
born of the Virgin Mary,
suffered under Pontius Pilate,
was crucified, died, and was buried.
He descended into hell.
On the third day he rose again.
He ascended into heaven,
and is seated at the right hand of the Father.
He will come again to judge the living and the dead.
I believe in the Holy Spirit,
the holy Catholic Church,
the communion of saints,
the forgiveness of sins,
the resurrection of the body,
and life everlasting. Amen.

The Apostles' Creed

A few years ago, I began reflecting upon the Apostles' Creed from the viewpoint of God's overflowing love. Everything God, our heavenly Creator, has done for us has been done out of love. And this is especially true as revealed to us through God the Son—through the life, death, and resurrection of Jesus—and through the coming of God, the Holy Spirit.

God's word to the people of Israel informs us, for example: "I have loved you with an everlasting love" (Jeremiah 31:13). And we all know so well the celebrated passage in John's Gospel: "God so loved the world that he gave his only Son, so that everyone who believes in him may not perish but may have eternal life" (3:16).

The Nature of Our Creeds

The creeds that we are most familiar with—the Nicene Creed, which we profess every Sunday at Mass, and the Apostles' Creed, with which one begins the rosary—are primarily professions of faith.

These creeds express the bare bones—and key doctrines—of our faith, to which we adhere mainly with our intellects, or so it sometimes seems. And yet we seem to know better. For we also understand that love is behind it all. And we know that "God is love," as John writes in 1 John 4:16, and that God does everything out of love.

We have all been instructed about the three theological virtues of faith, hope, and love. We need each of these virtues to live a fully spiritual life. Yet, St. Paul reminds us that love is the greatest gift: "…if I have all faith, so as to remove mountains, but do not have love, I am nothing" (see 1 Corinthians 13:2). Paul concludes later: "And now faith, hope, and love abide, these three; and the greatest of these is love." (13:13).

Deep down, we seem to understand that the doctrines or actions of God that we profess in our creeds are not simply intellectual truths but at their core are driven by love. God is all about love, and God's revelations and actions are motivated by love.

At this point, I invite you to reflect with me on the lines of the Apostles' Creed. For the sake of simplicity, we will use only the Apostles' Creed, which is the shorter profession of faith. As you, no doubt, know, the Nicene Creed, though more complex, follows the same basic sequence of teachings as is found in the Apostles' Creed.

It's All About Love

I believe in God the Father almighty,
creator of heaven and earth.

God did not create our immense universe and fill it with countless creatures simply to show off his power and wisdom, but out of love for all these creatures. On the sixth day of creation, God saw all that he had made and saw that it was very good.

It's hard to see how our Creator could see each of these creatures as "very good" without having created each of them with great love!

If you ponder Psalm 136:3–9 for a few moments, you will get a strong sense of the divine love that permeates all creatures:

> O give thanks to the Lord of lords,
>> for his steadfast love endures forever;
>
> who alone does great wonders,
>> for his steadfast love endures forever;
> who by understanding made the heavens,
>> for his steadfast love endures forever;
> who spread out the earth on the waters,
>> for his steadfast love endures forever;
> who made the great lights,
>> for his steadfast love endures forever;
> the sun to rule over the day,
>> for his steadfast love endures forever;
> the moon and stars to rule over the night,
>> for his steadfast love endures forever;

I believe in Jesus Christ, his only Son, our Lord.
He was conceived by the power of the Holy Spirit
and born of the Virgin Mary.
He suffered under Pontius Pilate,
was crucified, died, and was buried.
He descended to the dead.

Ponder the Gospel of John (the Last Supper Discourses):

> As the Father has loved me, so I have loved you; abide in my love. If you keep my commandments, you will abide in my love, just as I have kept my Father's commandments and abide in his love. I have said these things to you so that my joy may be in you, and that your joy may be complete. "This is my commandment, that you love one another as I have loved you." (John 15:9–12)

Now, ponder the Gospel of Luke and reflect on the amazing love with which Jesus hands over his body and blood in the form of bread and wine.

> Then he took a loaf of bread, and when he had given thanks, he broke it and gave it to them, saying, "This is my body, which is given for you. Do this in remembrance of me." And he did the same with the cup after supper, saying, "This cup that is poured out for you is the new covenant in my blood." (Luke 22:19)

On the third day he rose again.
He ascended into heaven,
and is seated at the right hand of the Father.
He will come again to judge the living and the dead.

To understand better the profound love hidden behind the death and resurrection of Jesus and his ascension into glory, simply reflect on our proclamation of "the mystery of faith" at the Eucharist: "Save us, Savior of the world, / for by your Cross and Resurrection / you have set us free" (*Roman Missal*). It is with immense love that Jesus sets us free by his cross and resurrection and then when he comes in glory to judge the living and the dead. And we will understand better the great mercy by which he will judge those of sincere heart when we ponder Jesus' great parable of the Prodigal Son. The father in that parable is filled with compassion when he catches sight of his son, embraces him, places the finest robe on him, and prepares a feast for him (see Luke 15:11–32).

I believe in the Holy Spirit,
the holy Catholic Church,
the communion of saints,
the forgiveness of sins,
the resurrection of the body,
and life everlasting. Amen

St. Paul says of the Holy Spirit, whose overflowing love is alive in all the mysteries listed above: "hope does not disappoint us, because God's love has been poured into our hearts through the Holy Spirit that has been given to us" (Romans 5:5). The love of God was truly poured out upon God's chosen ones the evening of that first Easter Sunday when the risen Jesus, passing through locked doors, stood in the midst of the disciples and said, "Peace be with you. As the Father has sent me, so I send you." Then Jesus breathed on them and said to them, "If you forgive the sins of any, they are forgiven them; if you retain the sins of any, they are retained" (John 20:21, 23). God's saving love and mercy is surely revealed in Jesus breathing forth the Spirit of love and forgiveness upon his disciples.

In the Acts of the Apostles, we see the same dynamic at work on the feast of Pentecost. After Jesus' ascension, the apostles and other disciples, and Mary the mother of Jesus, were gathered together in Jerusalem. "And suddenly from heaven there came a sound like the rush of a violent wind, and it filled the entire house where they were sitting. Divided tongues, as of fire, appeared among them, and a tongue rested on each of them. All of them were filled with the Holy Spirit and began to speak in other languages, as the Spirit gave them ability" (Acts 2:2–4).

Then Peter stood up and reminded those gathered what the prophet Joel proclaimed: "In the last days it will be, God declares, that I will pour out my Spirit upon all flesh… Then everyone who calls on the name of the Lord shall be saved" (Acts 2:17, 21). And later Peter, in his own words, professed: "This Jesus God raised up, and of that all of us are witnesses. Being therefore exalted at the right hand of God, and having received from the Father the promise of the Holy Spirit, he has poured out this that you both see and hear" (Acts 2:32–33).

The words of our traditional prayer, Come, Holy Spirit, provide a wonderful summary of the mystery of God's love: "Come, Holy Spirit, fill the hearts of your faithful. And enkindle in them the fire of your love." Indeed, it's important to remember always that behind our great Christian professions of faith lies the vast ocean of God's love.

The Glory Be

Glory be to the Father
and to the Son
and to the Holy Spirit,
as it was in the beginning
is now, and ever shall be
world without end. Amen.

The Glory Be

Most of us are well acquainted with this familiar prayer. It is known as a *doxology* (from the Greek word, *doxa*, meaning "glory"). A doxology is a liturgical expression of glory and praise to God.

Biblical scholars tell us that the Hebrew word for "glory," *kabod*, literally means "weight," and it leads us to the idea of glory. How does this happen? Well, the weight or heaviness of something suggests its importance or value—and ultimately its glory. However, one must always distinguish true glory from false glory.

Sometimes a person's wealth or high social position can be mistaken for that person's true glory, but it is not. For example, in our society we have heard of rich bankers and millionaires who have defrauded poor people out of their property or life savings. We see no true glory or real importance in such wealthy people. Even in the kings of the Old Testament, we have seen examples of glory that can be either true or terribly false or hollow. Great kings like David and Solomon, for example, had their moments of true glory (when they followed God's will) and of false glory (when they fell from grace). We get a hint of this in Matthew's Gospel, when Jesus says: "And why do you worry about clothing? Consider the lilies of the field, how they grow; they neither toil nor spin, yet I tell you, even Solomon in all his glory was not clothed like one of these" (6:28–29). True glory is a reflection of divine glory.

Examples of God's Glory
Divine glory is revealed in the radiance or light of the Lord's glory, as when God saved the Israelites at the Red Sea. "And the Egyptians shall know that I am the LORD, when I have gained glory for myself over Pharaoh, his chariots, and his chariot drivers" (Exodus 14:18). Or God's glory was manifested through the bright clouds and fire on top of Mount Sinai, as when Moses went up the mountain.

> The glory of the LORD settled on Mount Sinai, and the cloud covered it for six days; on the seventh day he called to Moses out of the cloud. Now the appearance of the glory of the Lord was like a devouring fire on the top of the mountain in the sight of the people of Israel. (Exodus 24:16–17)

This Divine glory is equally present in Christ. As we read in Hebrews, "[Christ] is the reflection of God's glory and the exact imprint of God's very being, and he sustains all things by his powerful word" (1:2). We get a glimpse of Christ's glory, moreover, in Matthew's Gospel, when Jesus is transfigured before Peter, James and John "on a high mountain." Jesus "was transfigured before them, and his face shone like the sun, and his clothes became dazzling white" (Matthew 17:2).

Surely this is a vision of Christ in glory, who never lost, of course, the glory he shared with the Father in the beginning.

Recall that at the Last Supper in John's Gospel (before his passion) Jesus said, "Father, the hour has come; glorify your Son so that the Son may glorify you, I glorified you on earth by finishing the work that you gave me to do. So now, Father, glorify me in your own presence with the glory that I had in your presence before the world existed..." (John 17: 1, 4–5).

Reciting the **Glory Be** *with Devotion*
We return to our doxology—to our familiar "Glory Be" prayer. Now that we are more enlightened as to the biblical meaning of the *glory* of God and have seen dramatic instances of it, we can recite the prayer with a growing awareness that the glory we give to God originally came from God and not the other way around. By opening ourselves to God's overflowing love and goodness and devoutly repeating this prayer, we share more deeply in the glorious life of God!

The Our Father

Our Father, who art in heaven,
hallowed by thy name,
thy kingdom come,
thy will be done
on earth as it is in heaven.
Give us this day our daily bread,
and forgive us our trespasses,
as we forgive those who trespass against us;
and lead us not into temptation,
but deliver us from evil.

CHAPTER THREE

The Our Father

Our Father, who art in heaven

At the end of my reflection on the previous prayer (the Glory Be), I spoke of opening ourselves to the overflowing love and goodness of God. I am convinced that the *"Our* Father" reveals that same abundant love and goodness. When Jesus proposes to his disciples that we use the word *Our* to address Our Father in heaven, Jesus is telling us how blessed we are in being allowed to claim the infinite, all good God as Our Father. That is indeed a gift from God that no creature can really earn. The word *our* also reminds us that we are persons in communion with each other. We are members of the larger human family as well as of the Body of Christ. The Our Father is the prayer of the church. We are reminded by Jesus that we are to pray as one large family or one church, not simply as individuals.

Then to discover, on top of this, that we may also call God *Father* really blows us away! Recall that a word Jesus sometimes uses for Father in the Gospel is *abba.* By using this word, Jesus is suggesting that this father is all the more approachable and loving. For *abba* suggests a father who is intimate, familiar, loving, forgiving, and personal—like a loving *dad.* Think again of the loving father of the Prodigal Son parable, who is ready to embrace and forgive the wayward son who returns in a repentant spirit.

"Who art in heaven" is not meant to suggest a place so much as God's majesty or divinity. God exits on a higher, much more glorious plain than we do. As the *Catechism of the Catholic Church* puts it, "Heaven, the Father's house, is the true homeland toward which we are heading and to which, already, we belong."[1]

> *Hallowed be thy name;*
> *thy kingdom come,*
> *thy will be done*
> *on earth as it is in heaven.*

The words *Hallowed by thy name*, are not to be interpreted as if *we* are the ones who hallow (or make holy) God's name. Rather God is the source of God's holiness. We do not cause God's holiness, but we recognize that God's abundant holiness is an essential quality of who God is and we praise and glorify God for it.

When we proclaim "Thy kingdom come," we are acknowledging God's redemptive presence in our world. When Jesus Christ walked among us, setting free the sick and the oppressed, he was the saving presence of God in our world. As *The United States Catholic Catechism for Adults* expresses it, "The Kingdom is Jesus Christ and all he means for us. The Kingdom is already here because of the redemption of Jesus Christ. But in another sense, it is 'not yet' here, since Christ's final transformation of individuals, society, and culture has yet to happen in its fullness."[2]

"Thy will be done" is another way of saying "thy kingdom come." God's will is not focused primarily on a whole bunch of strict moral rules that we must follow. God's larger focus is that we collaborate with Christ in spreading the kingdom of God, which is God's saving presence in this world. Timothy writes, "This is right and is acceptable in the sight of God our Savior, who desires everyone to be saved and to come to the knowledge of the truth" (1 Timothy 2:3–4). As the Gospel of John puts it, "Indeed, God did not send the Son into the world to condemn the world, but in order that the world might be saved through him" (John 3:17).

The three petitions of the Our Father—"hallowed by thy name, thy kingdom come and thy will be done"—deal with eschatological concerns. That is, they deal with the future of the church, the final events of human history, or what happens in the next life. The hallowing of God's name, the coming of God's kingdom, the accomplishment of God's will are all future-oriented ideas because they will come to total fulfillment only in heaven. In fact, the entire Our Father, though it has applications for right now, looks largely to the future. The remaining petitions of the Our Father, which we will look at now, have a strong future orientation.

> *Give us this day our daily bread,*
> *and forgive us our trespasses,*
> *as we forgive those who trespass against us;*
> *and lead us not into temptation,*
> *but deliver us from evil. Amen.*

"Our daily bread" suggests that we are praying primarily for what we need today. We are not to store up food or riches in a greedy fashion, nor are we to forget the poor, who often lack daily bread. We are to live in solidarity with other members of Christ's body and of the human family. Our thoughts about daily bread should also remind us of the Bread of Life and our participation in the Eucharist. We are to reflect as well on the future aspects of this bread. We do this by contemplating our joyful participation in the heavenly banquet, which will last forever and ever. This is surely a wonderful eschatological dimension of the Our Father and another sign of the overflowing bounty of God.

We ask that God forgive us our trespasses, as we forgive those who trespass against us. If we cannot forgive our neighbor, can we expect God to forgive us? This two-way kind of forgiveness makes sense. When we forgive our neighbor, that gesture frees *us* up at the same time. We become free of a grudge against another person—a grudge that can imprison us and eat us up from the inside. Such forgiveness of the other convinces us that it's also possible for our Father in heaven and others to forgive us. Such forgiveness goes a long way in setting us free—and setting the whole world free—of hatreds that ultimately do not allow the human community to move forward.

In the end, certainly, our God of abundant goodness and overflowing love "will not lead us into temptation, but will deliver us from evil." Thanks to Christ's life, death, and resurrection, our victory over death, temptation, and evil has already been won. Jesus sits victoriously at the right hand of the Father. All that remains for us is to walk on in faith and to say a heartfelt "Amen" for all that Christ has given us in the Our Father.

May our contemplating of the words and generous sentiments of the Our Father help to transform us into the image of the Risen Christ, who is "...the image of the invisible God, the firstborn of all creation" (Colossians 1:15).

God's Loving Will for Me
This is a reflection of my growing understanding of the words "Thy will be done on earth as it is in heaven." A gradual illumination of the meaning of these words has helped me to feel lighter of heart and more joyful as I grow older. In my younger years, God's will, at times, seemed dark and gloomy to me. In those years, when I prayed "Thy will be done," I thought of the words mainly in terms of *my* responsibility (and often a gloomy one at that) to obey a complicated set of moral laws and commandments so God would love me.

Today when I think of God's will, it is something quite different from the above. Now God's will nearly seem to glow with light. For I think of it, first of all, as God's *loving plan* to bring me and all God's people to healing and happiness. Today I see God's will as something much larger and more benevolent. I see it more as St. Francis saw it, namely, as God's desire to love us unconditionally and to lead us to abundance of life. Or to use St. Irenaeus's familiar words, "God's glory is the human person fully alive." Now when I pray, "Thy will be done," the words have a more joyful ring to them.

I still see, of course, a clear link between God's will and God's commandments. But God's commandments take on their true meaning only *after* I understand God's overarching and loving will that I be happy and fully alive. Obeying God's will is not, first of all, a dreary task of following a lot of rules and piling up good deeds so that God will love me and think well of me. God already loves me abundantly and wishes to save me.

My obeying, my moral task, therefore, is not a matter of bringing God's love into existence (God's love is already here!), but rather one of *responding* to that love. And I respond to it by joyfully, gratefully, and affectionately trying to follow God's commandments. For these commandments are now seen, not as cold disciplinary rules to burden my spirit, but as loving guidelines for discovering fullness of life. Obeying God's will is a matter of "response-ability" rather than of mere responsibility. Leading a good moral life is not the cause of God's loving me, but the *consequence* of God's loving me. God's gift of love comes before my task of responding to it, and not the other way around.

I believe this is what Jesus was trying to convey to us by his famous parable of the Pharisee and the tax collector (Luke 18:9–14). He shows the Pharisee sashaying to the front of the temple to tell God about the big stack of virtues he has piled up—fasting, paying tithes on all his income. It is a prayer of self-congratulation. Meanwhile, the tax collector barely dares to raise his eyes. He strikes his breast and prays, "O God, be merciful to me, a sinner." It is this humble man who went home justified, according to Jesus. It is not this human being's power that is so important, but God's. The most needed attitude on the tax collector's part is a humble openness and responsiveness to God's great goodness and mercy.

Lord Jesus, by reflecting on the wisdom contained in your parable, may we better understand God's loving will for us.

Anima Christi

Soul of Christ, sanctify me.
Body of Christ, save me.
Blood of Christ, inebriate me.
Water from the side of Christ, wash me.
Passion of Christ, strengthen me.
O Good Jesus, hear me.
Within your wounds, hide me.
Let me never be separated from you.
From the malignant enemy, defend me.
In the hour of my death, call me,
And bid me come to you,
That with your saints I may praise you
Forever and ever. Amen.

CHAPTER FOUR

Anima Christi

Before we begin meditating on the *Anima Christi*, ("Soul of Christ," in Latin), you will find this background helpful. Although the *Anima Christi* has been attributed at times to St. Ignatius of Loyola (1491–1556), historians agree that the prayer predates Ignatius by as much as a century and a half. There is a long tradition, however, that it was a favorite prayer of Ignatius. And for centuries it has often served as the opening prayer of his *Spiritual Exercises*.

I know a good number of people today who, in saying this prayer, affirm that it touches them on a profound emotional or mystical level. Don't be surprised if it does the same for you. My prayer is that the risen Christ becomes more present to your whole being as you grow in familiarity with this unusual prayer.

Although there are many translations of this prayer, the wording here is a rather literal translation of the original Latin. The prayer can be used very meaningfully as a eucharistic meditation, or to draw close to Christ at any time of day or night.

Soul of my Savior, sanctify me.

Jesus, Risen One, may your soul invade my whole being and make me holy. Breathe your Holy Spirit, the Sanctifier upon me, just as you breathed upon the first disciples after your resurrection. Set me free of sin and fill me with the holiness that fills your own soul.

Body of Christ, save me.

I open myself to your love. Embrace me with your healing and transforming power. Jesus, this prayer especially moves me after receiving your Body and Blood in Holy Communion or after Mass has ended. But I know the prayer is meaningful at any time. For I believe you are always standing at my door knocking (Revelation 3:20)—inviting me to open the door and have a heart-to-heart visit with you.

Blood of Christ, inebriate me.

You have redeemed me, Jesus, by your blood shed upon the cross. At the Eucharist, I receive that blood in the form of wine. Your burning love is so overwhelming that one feels intoxicated by the intensity of your care.

Water from the side of Christ, wash me.

Yes, Jesus, let the water flowing from your side cleanse me, as did the life-giving water which flowed over me at baptism. This saving stream never stops flowing through me—unless I separate myself from your love. You are the Vine, I am the branch. If I remain in you, your abundant life continues flowing into me. As St. Paul attests, "...it is no longer I who live, but it is Christ who lives in me. And the life I now live in the flesh I live by faith in the Son of God, who loved me and gave himself for me" (Galatians 2:20).

Passion of Christ, strengthen me.

It is your power and mercy that saves me and gives me strength, and not my own. As the psalmist says, "Unless the LORD builds the house, / those who build it labor in vain" (127:1). Help me to stay united with you and your passion, which reveals your saving love for me and all your people.

O Good Jesus, hear me. Within your wounds hide me.

There is something so mystical, and dare I say intimate, Jesus, in our hiding in those holy wounds through which we are saved. As Isaiah tells us, "by his bruises we are healed" (53:5). Draw us into this most loving mystery—this sacred fountainhead of our salvation!

Let me never by separated from you.

Loving Savior, this expresses, perhaps, the most central theme of *Anima Christi*. Keep reminding me that the best part of prayer is not so much in gaining information about you, O Jesus, as it is in growing into a closer love union with you. So, loving Savior, hold us close to you.

From the malignant enemy, defend me.

This line is similar to the closing line of that special prayer that you yourself taught us—the Our Father: "Lead us not into temptation, but deliver us from evil. Amen." We rely on your saving power, O Lord, to set us free of anything that might cause us to be separated from you and your Kingdom of saving love.

In the hour of my death, call me, and bid me come to you,
that with your saints I may praise you forever and ever.
Amen.
Jesus, I need your help to reach my final fulfillment in your
Kingdom. Stay with me to the end—until I can join in singing
your praises with all those saved by your love.

Broadening Our Scope: Shifting From "Me" to "Us"
Beginning with the heading: "O Good Jesus, hear me" (four
paragraphs above), you may have noticed how my reflections
on the *Anima Christi* began to stray away from the "me" and
"my" vocabulary of this very personal prayer, and I have
begun to use plural pronouns like "we" and "us" and "our."
The *Anima Christi*, in its original wording, is very much a personal prayer focused on our individual relationship with
Christ (and indeed we are indeed called to deepen our own
personal union with Christ). We also know from the changes
ushered into the church by the Second Vatican Council
(1962–1965) that we have been encouraged to come to more
communal ways of celebrating the sacraments and of praying
together as church. This in no way contradicts the importance
of respecting those times in our lives when the Holy Spirit calls
us to more personal experiences of prayer.

I have found it fruitful in my own praying of the *Anima*
Christ to alternate between the personal and the communal—
and I have heard others also speak very favorably of doing the
same. Perhaps you will find this fruitful as well. A number of
people I know have the prayer memorized and say the *Anima*
Christi first personally in the traditional form, as quoted at the
beginning of this meditation. Then afterwards they might say

it in the "us" and "our" form of the prayer, as quoted at the end of this meditation. In this way, they can include coworkers, family members, or a sick relative, dear friend, or loved one in the prayer. There are certain situations where I find it very fruitful to recite this prayer with a relative or special friend or even with a whole group of people. Thus in the same prayer, you can contemplate your personal love relationship and union with Christ and, at the same time, think, and pray lovingly for those in need.

Sometimes I wake up in the middle of the night or before dawn and am unable to sleep for maybe an hour or more. I sometimes find great peace and meaning in contemplating my union with Christ as well as with those I include in my prayer. Having memorized the *Anima Christi*, I go through the prayer, meditating on it phrase by phrase, perhaps while fingering rosary beads. At times, it becomes a profound mystical experience.

After all, the *Anima Christi* expresses nothing less than Christ's incredible love not only for me but also for any others (and all others) who come into my consciousness.

Lord Jesus, sanctify us all. May we never be separated from you and from those we love!

Anima Christi *for "Us"*

Before I present my "us" and "we" form of the *Anima Christi*, let me mention a few things. First of all, not everybody has to buy this version, although some of my friends and acquaintances have been using it for some time now, and with more than a little enthusiasm. If you tend to like traditional things, you may, of course, wish to stick with the traditional version.

For others who want to try the plural version, let me explain a bit. I have added a few additional words to the prayer (in four instances) which seem to enhance the prayer's meaning. The changes appear in the following four examples. Simply note the italicized words: "Let us never by separated from you *or from each other.*" "From the malignant enemy, defend us *and deliver us.*" "With your *angels* and saints *and all your creatures* we may praise you forever and ever. Amen."

The reasons for the changes in the first three instances are rather obvious to me. In the fourth instance, however, the addition of *and all your creatures* may seem puzzling to some. So here's my explanation. It is simply an effort to give a touch of Franciscan spirituality to this ancient and venerable prayer. St. Francis saw all creatures as his brothers and sisters. And his followers, more and more, are coming to believe that all these creatures are meant to share in God's glory in heaven along with all the humans who have been redeemed. After all, would St. Francis in his *Canticle of the Creatures* invite Brother Sun and Sister Moon and Stars, Brother Fire and Sister Water and Our Sister, Mother Earth to praise God with him on this earth, but not invite them to do the same in heaven? Think about it. I invite all who wish to continue your meditation on the *Anima Christi* in plural form. You can do so by praying the form below.

Anima Christi (plural form)
Soul of Christ, sanctify us.
Body of Christ, save us.
Blood of Christ, inebriate us.
Water from the side of Christ, wash us

Passion of Christ, strengthen us.
O Good Jesus, hear us.
Within your wounds, hide us.
Let us never be separated you or from each other.
From the malignant enemy, defend us and deliver us.
In the hour of our death, call us,
And bid us come to you,
That with your angels and saints and all your creatures
We may praise you forever and ever. Amen.

Come, Holy Spirit

Come, Holy Spirit, fill the hearts of your faithful,
and enkindle in them the fire of your love.
Send forth your Spirit, and they shall be created.
And you shall renew the face of the earth.

CHAPTER FIVE

Come, Holy Spirit

If we go in search for very first image of God's Spirit in the Bible, we find that image—"a wind from God"—in the second verse of Genesis: "In the beginning when God created the heavens and the earth, the earth was a formless void and darkness covered the face of the deep, while a wind from God swept over the face of the waters" (Genesis 1:1–2). *Ruah* is the Hebrew word for "wind," "breath," or "spirit," and any of these three words is a possible translation of *ruah*, depending on the circumstance. In any case, we see the wind, breath, or spirit of God sweeping over the primordial waters. This primal image suggests to us that the foremost role or activity of God's Spirit is that of presiding over the genesis (or birth) of new life. As we profess in the Nicene Creed, "We believe in the Holy Spirit...the giver of life."

Clearly symbolized by the spirit's sweeping over the primordial waters in the book of Genesis is the power of God's spirit to draw forth from the chaotic waters an orderly creation of new life. Henceforth, the spirit is present at each new burst of life. Note, for example, the "breath of life" image at the birth of Adam: "[T]hen the LORD God formed man from the dust of the ground, and breathed into his nostrils the breath of life; and the man became a living being" (Genesis 2:7).

There are countless other references to the Spirit of God in the Hebrew Scriptures, such as when the prophet Samuel anointed with oil the shepherd boy David (selected by God to be king), "...and the spirit of the LORD came mightily upon David from that day forward" (1 Samuel 16:13). Usually, such actions of the Spirit represent a new initiative—a new development or an entry of new life—in God's plans for the good of humanity.

The Holy Spirit in the New Testament
One of God's most dramatic creations of new life in the gospels comes about by way of the Incarnation of the eternal Word of God, Jesus Christ. It's the emergence of the new Adam, indeed, of a whole new creation. We should not be surprised to see the Holy Spirit, "the giver of life," profoundly involved in this mystery. When Mary asks how it can happen that she, a virgin, can bear a son who "will be called Son of the Most High," she is told by the angel: "The Holy Spirit will come upon you, and the power of the Most High will overshadow you; therefore the child to be born will be holy; he will be called, the Son of God" (see Luke 1:31–36).

Later, the baptism of Jesus is another great moment of new life, described in Mark's Gospel. It is certainly food for meditation: "And just as he was coming up out of the water, he saw the heavens torn apart and the Spirit descending like a dove on him. And a voice came from heaven, 'You are my Son, the Beloved; with you I am well pleased'" (Mark 1:10–11). The Holy Spirit in this scene is dramatically anointing Jesus as

Messiah. Spurred on by this new and abundant rush of life, Jesus is ready to embark on his public ministry, in which he will proclaim the Kingdom of God by word and deed.

But first the Holy Spirit drives Jesus into the desert for forty days, where he is tempted by Satan, in preparation for many new levels of life awaiting him through the power of the Spirit. For the rest of his earthly life, every action of Jesus will be done through the Holy Spirit. For example, Jesus returns from the desert to Galilee "filled with the power of the Spirit" (Luke 4:14) and he ends up in Nazareth, his hometown. There he goes into the synagogue, unrolls the scroll and reads this passage from Isaiah:

> The Spirit of the Lord is upon me,
>   because he has anointed me to bring good news to the
>   poor.
> He has sent me to proclaim release to the captives
>   and recovery of sight to the blind,
>   to let the oppressed go free,
> to proclaim the year of the Lord's favor."
>   And he rolled up the scroll, gave it back to the attendant, and sat down. The eyes of all in the synagogue were fixed on him. Then he began to say to them, "Today this scripture has been fulfilled in your hearing." All spoke well of him and were amazed at the gracious words that came from his mouth. They said, "Is not this Joseph's son?" (Luke 4:18–22)

The power of the Holy Spirit, so visible at Jesus' baptism and ensuing events, continues to guide him throughout his earthly life. Suffering and death will be part of this. Indeed, Jesus will compare his crucifixion and death to a baptism, which will lead him to an entry into new life by way of the resurrection. Recall that Jesus had asked James and John, the two apostles who were seeking a shortcut to glory, if they were ready to "be baptized with the baptism that I am baptized with" (Mark 10:38). Jesus was clearly referring to his passion and death on the cross.

Just as Jesus, after his baptism in the Jordan, rose up from the river "filled with the power of the Spirit," he now rises up from this new baptism and enters a whole new level of life—the resurrected life. "Two men in dazzling clothes," who appeared at the tomb (Luke 24:4–5), announce to the terrified disciples that Jesus now enjoys a new state of life and is not to be found in this place of death: "Why do you look for the living among the dead? He is not here, but has risen" (Luke 24:5–6). There is much to reflect upon in these passages.

Remembering Pentecost

We move now to Pentecost morning, as described in Acts. The disciples were all gathered in one place when, "suddenly from heaven there came a sound like the rush of a violent wind, and it filled the entire house where they were sitting. Divided tongues, as of fire, appeared among them, and a tongue rested on each of them. All of them were filled with the Holy Spirit and began to speak in other languages, as the Spirit gave them ability" (Acts 2:2–4). Peter stands up and addresses the Jews and all those staying in Jerusalem, saying, "[T]his is what was spoken through the prophet Joel: / 'In the last days it will be,

God declares, / that I will pour out my Spirit upon all flesh"
(Acts 2:16–17).

Each year, when we celebrate or remember Pentecost—or
whenever we recall the meaning of the Holy Spirit as the
"Giver of Life"—we are wise to assume an attitude of prayer-
ful waiting for the Holy Spirit who has been promised to us.
For that Spirit, who has been promised to us, is always ready
to guide us on our journey and to raise us to new levels of life.

Come, Holy Spirit
 Come, Holy Spirit, fill the hearts of your faithful,
  and enkindle in them the fire of your love.
 Verse: Send forth your Spirit, and they shall be created.
 Response: And you will renew the face of the earth.

*O God, you teach the hearts of the faithful by giving them
the light of your Holy Spirit. Grant to us that by your Spirit,
we may be truly wise, and always experience the joy of your
comforting presence. Through Christ our Lord. Amen.*

*Holy Spirit, we ask you to kindle in our hearts today the fire
of your love. We believe that your flaming love is always with
us, guiding us on our way. We imagine that each of us, like the
disciples of Jesus at Pentecost, has a small, tongue-like flame
of fire flickering above our heads. The flame symbolizes, O
gracious Spirit, your burning love within us. As the great apostle Paul assures the people of Corinth: "Or do you not know
that your body is a temple of the Holy Spirit within you, which
you have from God, and that you are not your own?" (1
Corinthians 6:19) and that "...God's love has been poured*

into our hearts through the Holy Spirit that has been given to us" (Romans 5:5). Ancient Spirit of God, we recall the image of you as a wind sweeping over the primordial waters of Genesis, to bring forth a new creation and a vast universe of new life. Here we are, Holy Spirit of God, standing humbly in your presence. Lead each of us to ever-richer levels of new life! Amen.

The Magnificat

My soul proclaims the greatness of the Lord;
my spirit rejoices in God my savior.
For he has looked upon his handmaid's lowliness;
Behold, from now on all ages will call me blessed.
The Mighty One has done great things for me,
and holy is his name.
His mercy is from age to age to those who fear him
He has shown might with his arm,
dispersed the arrogant of mind and heart.
He has thrown down the rulers from their thrones,
but lifted up the lowly.
The hungry he has filled with good things,
the rich he has sent away empty.
He has helped Israel his servant,
remembering his mercy,
according to his promise to our fathers,
to Abraham and his children forever.

CHAPTER SIX

The Magnificat

Mary's sublime prayer, the *Magnificat*, takes its name from the first word of the Latin translation of this song of praise. This explains why one sometimes runs into the translation: "My soul *magnifies* the Lord." Mary's Canticle is reminiscent of the hymn of praise which the Old Testament figure Hannah sang to the Lord after her state of childlessness was mercifully removed by God. Hannah, we know, joyfully bore her son Samuel, whom she dedicated to the Lord and who became a great prophet. In her song, Hannah proclaims, "My heart exults in the Lord" (1 Samuel 2:1) and in a later line she rejoices that the lord "raises the needy from the dust" (2:8). We see similar elements in Mary's song of praise.[1]

We ask the Spirit of God to enlighten our minds and hearts as we reflect on the lines of this great song that flow from the lips of Mary. The translation used here for Mary's Canticle (see Luke 1:46–55) is from the *New American Bible*.

> *My soul proclaims the greatness of the Lord;*
> *my spirit rejoices in God my savior.*

We find the context for Mary's song a few verses earlier in Luke's Gospel: The angel Gabriel has just told Mary that she will conceive and bear a son, Jesus, who will be called "Son of the Most High." He will be given "the throne of David his father and...of his kingdom there will be no end." Such glorious pronouncements did not cause Mary to swell with self-centered pride. Her heart was filled instead with worries and concerns. And yet she fully trusted "the Holy Spirit," who came upon her, as well as the "power of the Most High," who overshadowed her (see Luke 1:26–38). Although Mary had a profound sense of the goodness and "greatness of the Lord," she stayed in touch with her humble, finite, and frail humanity and creaturehood. Finally, Mary simply affirmed: "Behold, I am the handmaid of the Lord. May it be done to me according to your word" (1:38). Her spirit rejoiced, not in her own strength, but in the power of God's saving love.

For he has looked upon his handmaid's lowliness;
Behold, from now on will all ages call me blessed.
The Mighty One has done great things for me,
and holy is his name.
His mercy is from age to age to those who fear him

Mary understands, profoundly, where her salvation is coming from—not from *her virtue* but from *God's overflowing goodness*. If in the future all nations come to call her blessed, Mary knows, in all humility, that it is because of what the Mighty One has done for her, and not what she has done. In truth, all ages down the centuries have called her "blessed" and millions do so today each time they pray the Hail Mary. But the Mother of Jesus surely understands well the words of Psalm 127: "Unless the Lord build the house, they labor in vain who build it. Unless the Lord guard the city, in vain does the guard keep vigil."

He has shown might with his arm,
dispersed the arrogant of mind and heart.
He has thrown down the rulers from their thrones,
but lifted up the lowly.
The hungry he has filled with good things;
the rich he has sent away empty.

As was already noted in Hannah's hymn of praise, the Lord "raises the needy from the dust." So also in Mary's Canticle, we see God lifting "up the lowly" and throwing "down the rulers from their thrones." We see the same kind of reversals in Luke's gospel as a whole. Consider for example, Luke's series of blessings and woes in his Sermon on the Plain: "Woe to you who are filled now, for you will be hungry" (6:25). Or consider Luke 14:11: "Everyone who exalts himself will be humbled, but the one who humbles himself will be exalted." Surely, Mary would have somehow experienced these reversals in her son—his scourging, crucifixion, and death on the one hand—and his resurrection and his appearances to his disciples in glory, on the other. She would understand, moreover, the dynamics of St. Paul's Letter to the Philippians (2:8–9) where Paul speaks of Christ's own humbling, as well as exaltation:

"[Christ] humbled himself, becoming obedient to death,
even death on a cross.
Because of this, God greatly exalted him
and bestowed on him a name that is above every name...."

No doubt, Mary was already wrestling with these mysteries when she sang her Canticle—as well as decades later at the time of Jesus' suffering and death. And soon after, she would have known, of course, about his exaltation and rising into glory. More than this, she would know that the dual mysteries of humiliation and exaltation would still be significant challenges even later in the life of Jesus' disciples and in his Body, the church. In fact these are the struggles that all humans still deal with today.

He has helped Israel his servant,
remembering his mercy,
According to his promise to our fathers,
to Abraham and to his descendents forever.

My reflections on Mary's Canticle began with the observation that Mary's psalm of praise was similar to that which Hannah sang after she bore her son Samuel. Samuel, of course, was the great prophet who anointed both Saul (1 Samuel 10:1) and David (16:13). The prophet Samuel was thus a key figure in establishing the Davidic dynasty, which Jesus, the son of Mary, would become part of centuries later. When the angel Gabriel appeared to Mary in Luke's Gospel and told her she would give birth to Jesus, the angel said, "[He] will be called Son of the Most High and the Lord God will give him the throne of David his father, and he will rule over the house of Jacob forever" (Luke 1:32).

Luke indicates that Jesus is a successor or descendent of David through Joseph, Mary's husband. Luke does this in his genealogy of Jesus in which he says, "[Jesus] was the son, as was thought, of Joseph..." (see Luke 3:23). The Lucan genealogy also indicates that Jesus was a descendent of David (3:31) and of Abraham (3:34)—and it goes all the way back to "Adam, the son of God" (3:38).

Mary ends her Canticle with a sharp focus on Abraham, her father in faith—and the father in faith of all God's people. Abraham represents the beginnings of the story of Israel—a story which continues in Jesus Christ and his followers. A footnote at the beginning of St. Matthew's Gospel identifies "the coming of Jesus as the climax of Israel's history." Interestingly, Matthew identifies Jesus Christ as "the son of David, the son of Abraham" (Matthew 1:1). We go back now to Genesis and take a closer look at the Lord's call of Abraham: God said to Abram: "Go forth from the land of your kinsfolk and from your father's house to a land that I will show you. I will make of you a great nation, and I will bless you" (Genesis 12:1–2). As God later tells Abraham, "I will...make your descendents as countless as the stars of the sky and the sands of the seashore; ...and in your descendents [especially in the son of Mary], all the nations of the earth shall find blessing..." (22:17–18).

The greatness of Mary's Canticle is that it embraces the whole sweep of the story of Israel and that of the Incarnate Word—and the whole sweep of Mary's trust and complete openness to God. We are blessed in contemplating the words of Mary's amazing song!

The Hail Mary

Hail Mary, full of grace,
The Lord is with thee
Blessed art thou among women
And blessed is the fruit of thy womb, Jesus.
Holy Mary, mother of God,
Pray for us sinners,
Now and at the hour of our death. Amen.

CHAPTER SEVEN

The Hail Mary

The Hail Mary is one of the most popular and widely used prayers among Roman Catholics. To contemplate the words of this prayer is to explore several profound mysteries of our faith.[1]

Hail Mary, full of grace, the Lord is with thee.

The opening words of the prayer are the greetings of the angel Gabriel, who is God's own personal envoy, or mouthpiece. To call this young woman of Nazareth *full of grace* is to say that she is without sin for she has wholly given herself over to God who has come to dwell in her. The Lord will, indeed, be with her in a total and amazing way.

Blessed art thou among women.

In her *Magnificat*, Mary said, "Behold, from now on will all ages call me blessed." As I pointed out in my reflections on the *Magnificat* in the preceding chapter of this book (chapter eight): "In truth, all ages have called her 'blessed' and millions around the world do so today each time they pray the Hail Mary." And those of us who are saying, "Blessed art thou among women," as we pray the Hail Mary today, are doing the same thing—blessing her today as her cousin Elizabeth blessed her. Thus we see Elizabeth's words ("Blessed are you among women") and Mary's words ("All ages will call me blessed") coming true in our own times.

And blessed is the fruit of thy womb, Jesus.

These words were uttered by Elizabeth after her child, John the Baptist, leaped in her womb. The words contain an amazing truth: Mary is carrying the one who will become the Savior of the world. Can anyone have a more important mission in life than that given to Mary? And yet, you and I (ordinary human beings) are given the same mission. Yes, in many ways—through baptism, through the Eucharist, through prayer and through God's grace—we (ordinary Christians) have been given the same mission as Mary. Yes, Mary's mission and our mission to carry Christ into the world is the same.

Holy Mary, Mother of God.

This title has its source in the earliest days of the church. Mary is the Mother of God because she is the mother of Jesus, who is both truly divine and truly human. This doctrine was defined by the Council of Ephesus in AD 431. In the Eastern Church, Mary is called *Theotokos*, or "Birth-giver of God," which is sometimes translated "God-bearer." In Luke's Gospel, the angel Gabriel announces to Mary: "Behold, you will conceive in your womb and bear a son, and you shall name him Jesus" (Luke 1:31). In response, Mary says, "Behold, I am the handmaid of the Lord. May it be done to me according to your word" (Luke 1:38). Mary's humble response is her "yes" to accept God's plan to save the world by becoming the mother of Jesus, the Messiah.

Pray for us sinners,
now and at the hour of our death. Amen.

Mary, in your own life journey, you personally witnessed the suffering and death of your own son at the foot of the cross. Certainly, you grieved intensely and prayed fervently for Jesus during those painful moments. And as our mother, may you intercede fervently for us at the time of our dying—and welcome us into God's kingdom. Amen. Mother Mary, the words of this wonderful prayer have been said in your honor down the centuries. Help us and nurture us, that we might generously accomplish our own mission in the light of your own grace-filled example. Amen.

The Canticle of the Creatures

Most High, all-powerful, all good, Lord
All praise is yours, all glory, all honor
And all blessing.
To you, alone, Most High, do they belong.
No mortal lips are worthy
To pronounce your name.
All praise be yours, my Lord,
through all that you have made,
And first my lord Brother Sun,
Who brings the day; and light you give to us through him.
How beautiful is he, how radiant in all his splendor!
Of you, Most High, he bears the likeness.
All praise be yours, my Lord,
through Sister Moon and Stars;
In the heavens you have made them, bright
And precious and fair.
All praise be yours, my Lord,
through Brothers Wind and Air,
And fair and stormy, all the weather's moods,
By which you cherish all that you have made.
All praise be yours, my Lord, through Brother Fire,

Through whom you brighten up the night.
How beautiful is he, how merry!
Full of power and strength.
All praise be yours, my Lord,
through Sister Earth, our Mother,
Who feeds us in her sovereignty and produces
Various fruits with colored flowers and herbs.
All praise be yours, my Lord,
through those who grant pardon
For love of you; through those who endure
Sickness and trial.
Happy those who endure in peace,
By you, Most High, they will be crowned.
All praise be yours, my Lord, through Sister Death,
From whose embrace no mortal can escape.
How dreadful for those who die in sin!
How lovely for those found in Your Most Holy Will.
The second death can do them no harm.
Praise and bless my Lord, and give him thanks,
And serve him with great humility.

CHAPTER EIGHT

The Canticle of the Creatures

Historians have credited St. Francis of Assisi with composing the first great poem in Italian—a poem or hymn that bears the title *The Canticle of the Creatures* (also known as *The Canticle of Brother Sun*). In this hymn St. Francis invites all his brother and sister creatures—whether minerals, plants, or animals—to praise their Creator. These creatures include "Brother Sun" and "Sister Moon," "Brother Fire" and "Sister Water," as well as "Sister Earth our Mother," with all her various fruits and colored flowers.

For years, I have asked myself why—*why did Francis do this?* Deep down, I wondered: What intuition prompted Francis to address all creatures as "brothers" and "sisters"? Over thirty years ago, I concluded that Francis came to the conviction that *all creatures form one family of creation.* Indeed, this view of St. Francis is reflected—and also immortalized—in his *Canticle of Brother Sun.*

We will meditate on St. Francis' Canticle in segments. Although the Canticle is a very spontaneous poem or prayer flowing from the heart of Francis, it falls into distinguishable segments. For example, the first six lines of the canticle, presented below, are devoted to God alone. Our exalted Creator deserves first place in our reverence and high praise. And so, we do well to imitate St. Francis by contemplating our Most High God and offering "all praise" and "all glory" and "all honor" to this wonderful God, who created us all!

Most High, all-powerful, all good, Lord
All praise is yours, all glory, all honor
And all blessing.
To you, alone, Most High, do they belong.
No mortal lips are worthy
To pronounce your name.

In the next nineteen-line segment of the canticle, we focus on the various "brother" and "sister" creatures God has made. We praise God for their beauty and preciousness and for the way they reflect God's own goodness. It is fitting therefore that we embrace these creatures as brothers and sisters and as members of the same family to which you and I also belong.

All praise be yours, my Lord, through all that you have made,
And first my lord Brother Sun,
Who brings the day; and light you give to us through him.
How beautiful is he, how radiant in all his splendor!
Of you, Most High, he bears the likeness.
All praise be yours, my Lord, through Sister Moon
and Stars;
In the heavens you have made them, bright
And precious and fair.
All praise be yours, my Lord, through Brothers Wind
and Air,
And fair and stormy, all the weather's moods,

By which you cherish all that you have made.
All praise be yours, my Lord, through Brother Fire,
Through whom you brighten up the night.
How beautiful is he, how merry! Full of power and strength.
All praise be yours, my Lord, through Sister Earth,
our Mother,
Who feeds us in her sovereignty and produces
Various fruits with colored flowers and herbs.

Some time after St. Francis wrote and joyfully sang the original lines of the Canticle, he composed the following five lines to help resolve a dispute that had arisen between the mayor of Assisi and the bishop. St. Francis asked a friar to sing these lines in the presence of the two men so they might be reconciled. And, indeed, a peaceful reconciliation did take place. These lines also inspire us today to seek reconciliation with one another out of love for God. They will also lead us to peace and many blessings from the Most High.

All praise be yours, my Lord, through those who grant pardon
For love of you; through those who endure
Sickness and trial.
Happy those who endure in peace,
By you, Most High, they will be crowned.

Finally, Francis, not many days before he saw his own death approaching, added the following seven lines to his great *Canticle of the Creatures.*

All praise be yours, my Lord, through Sister Death,
From whose embrace no mortal can escape.
How dreadful for those who die in sin!

How lovely for those found in Your Most Holy Will.
The second death can do them no harm.
Praise and bless my Lord, and give him thanks,
And serve him with great humility.

Throughout this canticle, we have seen how Francis saw God's goodness, radiance, and beauty in all creatures. He saw them, indeed, as benevolent friends—as brothers and sisters—as family. And now even *death itself* becomes "Sister Death" for Francis, and thus takes on friendly and even "sisterly" aspects. For who of us is afraid of our own sister? Indeed, under usual circumstances we are not afraid of our sister. And so, neither does Francis see *this* sister as threatening to him. In fact, according to Thomas of Celano, the first biographer of the saint, St. Francis went "joyfully to meet [death]" and "invited it to make its lodging with him. According to Celano (2, CLXIII, 217), Francis said "Welcome, my sister death!"

We all owe a great debt to St. Francis of Assisi and to his *Canticle of the Creatures* for leading us to the conviction that all brother and sister creatures make up one family under God's loving care! May all these wonderful creatures continue to inspire us to lift our hearts upward to God in this glorious prayer of praise!

St. Francis' Prayer
Before the Crucifix

Most High
glorious God,
enlighten the darkness
of my heart.
Give me
right faith,
sure hope
and perfect charity.
Fill me with understanding
and knowledge
that I may fulfill
your command.

St. Francis' Prayer
Before the Crucifix

I have often reflected on this prayer, which—as Franciscan scholars attest—is indeed a prayer composed by St. Francis himself. And each time I pray it, I am more and more convinced that it reveals the authentic heart of St. Francis.

> *Most High,*
> *Glorious God,*
> *enlighten the darkness*
> *of my heart.*

Francis' prayer does not start with "Woe is me" or some dark misery of the soul. Rather it begins focused on the glory and sublime beauty of God.

By just praying the words in a spirit of praise, our hearts grow lighter and we feel swept up into the glorious presence of God! The prayer starts with words of praise! Praise has a way of lifting us out of our self-absorption and anxiety. Praise and thanksgiving help enlighten the darkness of my heart.

For some reason, I'm pleased that Francis uses the word *heart,* rather than *mind,* when he prays: "Enlighten the darkness of my heart." The word *mind* takes us too much into our

heads. And that is not the real St. Francis. *Heart* is very much
St. Francis. *Heart* suggests the complexities of human love and
the mystery of one's innermost longing—with all its related
joys and sorrows.

The heart of Francis was very much attuned to the full mystery of God's overflowing love. Once, while praying in a solitary place, Francis had a vision of Christ looking at him from
the cross with such burning love that "his soul melted,"
according to his biographer, St. Bonaventure (1221–1274). We
can only believe that, after this soul-melting event, every time
Francis prayed before a crucifix, he would reexperience a similar outpouring of God's incredible love.

Give me
right faith

When Francis says "right faith," this somehow evokes this
same heart-transforming vision of God's overflowing love, a
love whereby God holds nothing back from us! That's the kind
of *right faith* that Francis—as well as you and I—are pleading
for in this prayer. And does not this *right faith*—which is
focused upon the glorious revelation of God's total self-giving
and infinite love—*enlighten the darkness of our hearts?*

Sure hope

We pray with Francis for the "sure hope" that flows from
"right faith." And where does this *"sure hope"* reveal itself to
us more fully than in the Resurrection of Jesus? The disciples
literally witnessed *sure hope*, when the risen Christ appeared
to them on that first Easter Sunday. Consider especially the
apostle Thomas in this regard. The risen Jesus so illumined this

apostle's doubt-darkened heart on that day that Thomas, in adoration, proclaimed without hesitation: "My Lord and my God!"

and perfect charity.

Just as Francis sees Jesus on the cross handing himself over to Francis and to the whole human family with a total, perfect love, so Francis asks that he may receive the same kind of "perfect charity." This will enable Francis to respond to God's love with the same kind of total generosity. Francis asks further for Christ to "fill me with understanding and knowledge that I may fulfill your command." This "command" is really God's glorious plan that all God's children persevere in the love of Christ and some day rise with Christ into God's all-loving embrace.

The Cross of San Damiano

Early Franciscan documents of the thirteenth century indicate that the crucifix before which St. Francis was praying (in this prayer) was none other than the famous crucifix hanging in the little chapel of San Damiano, near Assisi. This beloved crucifix, familiar to followers of St. Francis worldwide, is known as the San Damiano cross. If you don't have an image of it, an online search will yield many examples. The cross is a great aid for meditation.

If you look closely at the body of Christ as painted on this cross, you will see that it is not a bloody body or one twisted in anguish. Rather his body is quite luminous, as if it were already his risen body, radiating the fullness of God. Instead of a crown of thorns, moreover, Christ's head is surrounded by a glorious halo. And his body with outstretched arms appears to be ascending to heaven. In short, the image clearly suggests that it represents Jesus rising into glory.

If, indeed, this was the image of Christ which St. Francis was pondering as this prayer arose in his heart, it makes perfectly good sense that Francis would address Jesus as "Most high glorious God!" For all the signs of heavenly glory are there.

O glorious God of overflowing love, enlighten the darkness of our hearts!

The Stigmata of St. Francis

The Greek word *stigma* means "a scar left by a hot iron: brand." *Stigmata*—the plural form of the same Greek word—can also mean "bodily marks resembling the wounds of the crucified Christ." This provides a basic background for understanding the mysterious phenomenon of the stigmata in Christian history.

I begin my reflections on the mystery of the stigmata by confessing that the first person I think of as having such bodily marks, apart from Jesus, is St. Francis of Assisi, who died in 1226. As the founder of the Franciscan Order, St. Francis is certainly a primary shaper of Franciscan spirituality. St. Francis therefore is a preeminent focal point in helping us contemplate the meaning of the wounds of Christ and of his own wounds and thus to come to a Franciscan understanding of suffering.

The Crucified Christ Appears to Francis

On two separate, dramatic occasions, Francis had a vision of Jesus, wounded in hands, feet and side, suffering on a cross. If we look carefully at the two visions, we will see them as closely interrelated. Both visions are described in St. Bonaventure's *Life of St. Francis*. It's helpful to remember that Bonaventure as a Franciscan theologian and spiritual writer often described God as a God of overflowing goodness and love.

The first vision (which we discussed briefly in our previous meditation) happened to Francis shortly after his conversion from a rather worldly life. After that experience, Bonaventure tells us that "One day, while Francis was praying in a secluded spot and became totally absorbed in God through his extreme fervor, Jesus Christ appeared to him fastened to the cross. Francis *soul melted* at the sight, and the memory of Christ's passion was so impressed on the innermost recesses of his heart that from that hour, whenever Christ's crucifixion came to mind, he could scarcely contain his tears and sighs."[1]

Bonaventure points out that from that time on Francis began "rendering humble service to lepers with human concern and devoted kindness....He visited their houses frequently, and generously distributed alms to them and with great compassion kissed their hands and their mouths."[2]

Francis' Vision on Mount La Verna
About two years before his death, St. Francis had a second vision of Christ fastened to the cross. Here is how St. Bonaventure sets the scene in his *Life of St. Francis*:

> On a certain morning about the Feast of the Exaltation of the Cross [September 14], while Francis was praying on the mountainside, he saw a Seraph with six fiery and shining wings descend from the height of heaven. And when in swift flight the

Seraph had reached a spot in the air near the man of God, there appeared between the wings the figure of the a man crucified, with his hands and feet extended in the form of a cross and fastened to a cross. Two of the wings were lifted above his head, two were extended for flight and two covered his whole body.

When Francis saw this, he was overwhelmed and his whole body was flooded with a mixture of joy and sorrow. He rejoiced because of gracious way Christ looked upon him under the appearance of the Seraph, but the fact that he was fastened to a cross *pierced his soul with a sword* of compassionate sorrow.[3]

This is a good place to say a word about the Seraph. Seraphs are those angels closest to God, burning with love as they bow before the Most High God, shouting "Holy, holy, holy!" (see Isaiah 6:2–3). Their fiery wings, as depicted here, suggest the flaming intensity of God's love that Christ communicated to Francis, which in turn, set Francis' heart afire. The word *seraphic* is often used to describe Francis's passionate style of relating to God and is often applied to the whole Franciscan Order, which is sometimes called the Seraphic Order.

The Meaning of the Stigmata

As suggested earlier, St. Francis is an important key for us in unlocking the meaning of Christ's stigmata. September is a good month to contemplate the meaning of the stigmata for any of us who consider ourselves followers of St. Francis. As many of us know, Franciscans celebrate the feast of the Stigmata of St. Francis of Assisi each year on September 17, which is an estimated date of his receiving the wounds of Christ at Mount La Verna in 1224, two years before his death. Just as St. Francis in his vision of the crucified Christ saw in the wounds of Jesus an incredible outpouring of God's love upon him, so we, too, are called to contemplate that vision in the same spirit.

When St. Francis saw in his vision of the Crucified Christ the incredible outpouring of God's love upon him, he was inspired to respond with the same kind of overflowing love. We too contemplate that vision and try to respond in the same spirit.

Lord, Jesus Christ, we praise you and adore you. Like Francis, we are amazed that you held nothing back from us in pouring yourself out for us so totally through your holy wounds on the cross. We ask you to breathe forth your Holy Spirit into us and set our hearts on fire, so that, with the Spirit's help, we might respond more fully to you. Amen.

The Franciscan Coat of Arms

CHAPTER TEN

The Franciscan Coat of Arms

If you go to any of our Franciscan friaries, churches, or convents, you will almost always find painted somewhere, hanging on a wall or visible over a doorway the Franciscan coat of arms. This holds true around the world as well as through the centuries.

The Franciscan coat of arms often consists of a cross with two arms crossing each other and nailed to a cross—or at least with a cross in the background. One arm is that of Christ; the other is that of St. Francis of Assisi. This image is a key identification badge for those who consider themselves followers of St. Francis.

This Franciscan coat of arms is an image worthy of our contemplation. The image is a true expression of both Jesus' and Francis' fervent style of love. We see in Jesus' crucified hand, first of all, God's incredible overflowing love for us. In Francis' wounded hand, in turn, we see the incredibly loving response of St. Francis to the burning love of God, who first loved us. This is indeed something to ponder. All in all, the Franciscan coat of arms is a wonderful expression of the Franciscan (or Seraphic) style of love. Though we seldom live up to this ideal, it calls us to something rare and splendid!

Lord Jesus, you said, "No one has greater love than this: to lay down one's life for one's friends." Help us to contemplate the amazing intensity of your love, as symbolized by your crucified hand. Help us also to imitate you more fully who first loved us and to imitate St. Francis who responded so fervently to the love so lavishly pour out upon him. Amen.

The Way of the Cross

First Station: Jesus Is Condemned to Death
Second Station: Jesus Accepts His Cross
Third Station: Jesus Falls the First Time
Fourth Station: Jesus Meets His Sorrowful Mother
Fifth Station: Simon Helps Jesus Carry the Cross
Sixth Station: Veronica Wipes the Face of Jesus
Seventh Station: Jesus Falls the Second Time
Eighth Station: Jesus Speaks to the Weeping Women
Ninth Station: Jesus Falls the Third Time
Tenth Station: Jesus Is Stripped of His Garments
Eleventh Station: Jesus Is Nailed to the Cross
Twelfth Station: Jesus Dies on the Cross
Thirteenth Station: Jesus Is Taken Down from the Cross
Fourteenth Station: Jesus Is Laid into the Tomb

CHAPTER ELEVEN

The Way of the Cross

We come to walk with you, Jesus, confident that following your journey to the cross will lead us closer to God's loving heart. In your bruised face and wounded body, we have a powerful image of God's care for us. Saints like Francis of Assisi shed streams of tears as they contemplated the amazing outpouring of God's love.

First Station: Jesus Is Condemned to Death
Jesus' way of life put him on a collision course with the powerful and mighty of his day. His "crime" was to take seriously the mission described in Isaiah: "The Spirit of the Lord has anointed me to bring glad tidings to the poor....to proclaim liberty to captives and recovery of sight to the blind, to let the oppressed go free..." (61:1). Jesus' challenge to those in positions of power led to his condemnation.

Second Station: Jesus Accepts His Cross
Jesus must now carry the instrument of torture through the streets of Jerusalem. Some future day—because of his ultimate triumph over death—Jesus cross will become a badge of glory. But on Good Friday itself—for Jesus the convicted criminal—the cross was a badge of shame. Yet in loving fidelity to his

Father's plan and out of compassion for humanity, he accepts this huge challenge. Help us, Jesus, to walk in the same Spirit!

Third Station: Jesus Falls the First Time
Weakened by torture and fatigue, Jesus collapses under the cross. Now the "God-man" fully tastes the frailty and poverty of the human condition. He shares the helplessness of those who come face-to-face with their own human limitations: the spouse who helplessly watches a wife or husband die of cancer; a youth overwhelmed by divorce in the family; a human rights worker sitting ten years in a prison for a cause that seems to all others for naught.

Fourth Station: Jesus Meets His Sorrowful Mother
What do their eyes say as they look at each other, this mother and son meeting on the Savior's death march? Love certainly shines in the eyes of both—and a deep faith that God is present in their struggles. God throws down the rulers from their thrones but lifts up the lowly (Luke 1:52). Mary's loving eyes assure Jesus of this. Even though she would like to run away from this heart-piercing moment, Mary is fully present to Jesus. She walks in solidarity with him and with all her oppressed children.

Fifth Station: Simon Helps Jesus Carry the Cross
Jesus is encouraged by another human being. We are reminded of Jesus' own words that care shown to others, even strangers, is care shown to Christ (see Matthew 25:31–46). When we feed or shelter another woman or man, we are doing the same for Christ. When we visit someone who is sick, we are showing a similar kindness to Christ. When we struggle to change

unjust social structures—such as racism, sexism, and other forms of oppression—we help alleviate the suffering of millions of others who embody Christ.

Sixth Station: Veronica Wipes the Face of Jesus
Veronica steps forward to gently press her veil to the bleeding and dirty face of this convicted outcast. What will people say? Won't they link her with the rejects, lawbreakers and those living on the fringes of society? Yet, she will not be intimidated. She sees profound dignity even in the disfigured face of this condemned man. She rejects the standards of this world which see only the rich and glamorous as worthy of attention. In the faces of the poor and the downtrodden, she sees the very face of God.

Seventh Station: Jesus Falls the Second Time
The cross that Jesus carries and which once more crushes him to the ground is the ugly burden of the sins of many. Jesus would not be on his way to a cruel death if Pilate had been less self-seeking, if religious leaders had been less envious, if Peter had been less cowardly or if the whole human race, from Adam and Eve to you and me, had been more open to God's grace. It is we human beings acting contrary to God's will— not God—who are responsible for so much of the suffering and poverty of this world.

Eighth Station: Jesus Speaks to the Weeping Women
The weeping women who follow Jesus remind us of the courageous role of many women during Jesus' passion. It is a role many women have borne throughout the centuries, in a world and a church that has too often not welcomed their

contributions. Jesus is less concerned about justifying his innocence than about being sensitive to the plight of the weeping women. He wants all persons to reach full potential as human beings created in God's image. That is an important part of his mission—and of ours, too.

Ninth Station: Jesus Falls the Third Time
We understand these moments of defeat. We know how hard it is to get up some mornings to face work or school, especially when severe challenges await us. We may face family problems, addiction, or perhaps we can not resign ourselves to some deep personal loss or failure. It is the dark night of the soul. Facedown on the ground, we remember that God's Spirit is in us. And drinking deeply of it, like Jesus, we choose to be faithful to the end.

Tenth Station: Jesus Is Stripped of His Garments
Jesus' clothes are torn from him. This irreverence is not simply against his body but against the sacredness, integrity, and privacy of his inner person. In a sense, he is stripped of his human dignity. It's not unlike being a victim of human exploitation or perhaps of sexual abuse. In a deeper sense, however, Jesus' dignity does not depend upon the quality of his clothing or upon the decisions of those who would exploit him, but upon God. He stands before his persecutors with a dignity and grandeur that no one can take away.

Eleventh Station: Jesus Is Nailed to the Cross
Because of Jesus' incredible brand of mercy, the very nails that we drive into his hands and feet are driving away our guilt. Jesus really *lived* his teachings about forgiveness: "Love your

enemies and pray for those who persecute you" (Matthew 5:44). "Do good to those who hate you" (Luke 6:27). Jesus' love is so pure and generous that he seeks only to build up others, no matter what they do to him. If someone throws a lance into his heart, he wants the blood flowing from it to wash away that person's sin. Perhaps, Jesus' greatest gift to us is his forgiveness. For without it we are locked in permanent alienation from God and from each other.

Twelfth Station: Jesus Dies on the Cross
As he dies on the cross, Jesus shares the desolation of countless people who see their dreams collapsing before them. He feels abandoned even by God. But in the end he dies the way he lived—with total trust in his Father's love. Out of the darkness of defeat comes the world's redemption. We can already proclaim the good news: "Lord, by your cross and resurrection, you have set us free. You are the Savior of the world." Even though the world will not be completely healed and reconciled within history, but only when Christ comes again, Jesus has broken the hold of sin and death over us. And our liberation has begun!

Thirteenth Station: Jesus Is Taken Down from the Cross
The lifeless, battered body of Jesus is lowered into Mary's arms. This human shell had contained the most honorable life that ever lived. With Mary we can confidently proclaim, "The Mighty One...has thrown down the rulers from their thrones and has lifted up the lowly" (Luke 1:52). It has been said that we can take from this life, nothing that we have selfishly gained—the illusory trappings of status, power or wealth—

only what we have given. And Jesus has given the most of all: a whole life dedicated to healing people and honoring his Father.

Fourteenth Station: Jesus Is Laid into the Tomb
Though the body of Jesus has been placed into a tomb, we know that his saving work has not been stopped. On the contrary, in three days God will raise him up in glory, and he will go before us into Galilee and every place where his mission is to flourish. We can embrace no greater challenge than to plunge into the mission of the risen Lord and be witnesses of his liberating presence in our world.

Lord Jesus, the same power of God which has raised you to new life raises us also. We believe that you remain with us always, completing your mission with our help and through the power of your Holy Spirit.

I See His Blood Upon the Rose

I see his blood upon the rose
And in the stars the glory of his eyes,
His body gleams amid eternal snows,
His tears fall from the skies.

I see his face in every flower;
The thunder and the singing of the birds
Are but his voice—and carven by his power
Rocks are his written words.

All pathways by his feet are worn,
His strong heart stirs the ever-beating sea,
His crown of thorns is twined with every thorn,
His Cross is every tree.

—Joseph Mary Plunkett[1]

| | |

I See His Blood Upon the Rose

Born in Dublin in 1887, Joseph Plunkett wrote many poems of rare mystical force. Plunkett was one of the signers of the Proclamation of the Irish Republic and was imprisoned by the British army. He was executed in 1916 for his part in the 1916 Rising. Shortly before his execution on the morning of May 4, he married his fiancée, Grace Clifford, in the jail's chapel. Plunkett was twenty-eight years old.

Because of his great love for the Incarnate Word and the Word's close connection to all created things, Plunkett seemed to see Christ's destiny and great love for us as forever entwined with this earth and this universe. In Joseph Plunkett's poetic lines, we see much to contemplate, for the lines and images of this poem seem to overflow with God's immense love for us.

I see his blood upon the rose

When we gaze at a rose or any other part of this universe, we see not only the individual beauty of the rose, precious and awesome in its own right. We contemplate also the intensity of God's care lavished upon that rose and upon the universe itself—an intensity revealed in Christ's all-out, self-giving love, in his love spilt for us on the cross.

And in the stars the glory of his eyes

In the stars, we see not only the glory of Jesus' heroic death and total self-giving. We see also the glory of his risen body and his death-conquering gaze.

His body gleams amid eternal snows

When we look at snow-capped mountains or other snowy vistas, we might see glimpses of Christ's pale body, as when taken down from the cross—or his glorified, transfigured body shining brighter than snow.

His tears fall from the skies

Again behind the everyday processes of nature such as a spring shower, we can't help seeing the love of our Great Lover—and the tears he shed over Jerusalem or later during his agony in the garden.

I see his face in every flower

Every flower, indeed, everything in the universe, reminds us of Christ. As Paul tells the Colossians (1:16), "All things were created through him and for him." We recall, too, that St. Francis saw in the beauty of a flower the one who is Beauty itself.

The thunder and the singing of the birds
Are but his voice

Singing birds and all other sounds of nature communicate one thing: God's great love for us.

And carven by his power
Rocks are his written words

Christ, the Word made flesh, is truly intermingled with the universe. The created world itself is a reflection of the Word, through whom "all things came to be" (John 1:3).

All pathways by his feet are worn

At the Incarnation, God made this world his home. Every path, trail, and road of this earth has taken on elevated dignity and meaning because the God-Man walked on every kind of path, and also because of that special path Christ took while accomplishing his mission on earth, namely, the pathway we call—the Way of the Cross.

His strong heart stirs the ever-beating sea

In the sea pounding against the jagged coast, we get glimpses of Christ's mighty heart pounding with love for us.

His crown of thorns is twined with every thorn

Every thorn is somehow intertwined with Christ's crown of thorns. Indeed, in every created thing we see Christ's saving love.

His cross is every tree

Behind every tree, we can see the Creator's unconditional love.

A Meditation on St. Anthony
and the Child Jesus

CHAPTER THIRTEEN

A Meditation on St. Anthony and the Child Jesus

If there is anything I've learned from visiting churches and Catholic missions throughout the world, it's that the image of St. Anthony and the child Jesus is a popular work of art enjoyed by many people in many places. From the Philippines to Guatemala, Anthony and the Child Jesus can be found wherever Catholic missionaries have carried the Good News— even into the most remote regions of the world.

For years I thought that such statues and images of Anthony holding the Child Jesus were little more than quaint pieces of sentimental art. Not looking for a deeper meaning in this familiar image, I seldom asked others or myself, "*Why* is St. Anthony presented this way?" In recent years, however, I've taken a whole different tack. I've concluded that this popular image has developed in the Franciscan and Roman Catholic tradition for some profound reason. I began wondering whether this image of St. Anthony might be actually tapping into something very important in our Franciscan and Christian tradition.

Unraveling the Meaning of a Dream

As I began to contemplate this familiar image a little more deeply, it struck me that such an exploration was like trying to understand a mysterious or strange dream we've experienced during the night. We wake up the next morning and wonder, "Now what was that strange dream all about?" I have come to believe that the dream-like image of Anthony with the child has emerged from the inner or subconscious life of the church—and that it may hold profound meanings for us.

Following in the Footsteps of St. Francis

By looking historically at the image of St. Anthony with the child Jesus, we learn a number of things. First of all, we notice that Anthony is wearing a Franciscan habit. Seeing Anthony as a true son of St. Francis and a part of the Franciscan tradition is very important. For example, as a committed member of Francis' Order and a brilliant scholar, Anthony would have known well the spirit, teachings, values, and dramatic actions of Francis. Like the other friars, Anthony would have surely heard about Francis' famous celebration of Christmas near Greccio, Italy, in 1223.

On that occasion, St. Francis had people come to Midnight Mass in a cave near Greccio, Italy, where there was an ox and an ass and a manger filled with straw. Anthony would have been well aware of the story going around that the Christ child appeared in the straw and that Francis held the child in his arms. How interesting! The image of the baby Jesus in the arms of St. Anthony is a kind of copycat image amazingly similar to St. Francis holding the Child Jesus during the midnight Christmas Mass in Greccio.

Even more important is the attitude or theology behind the story. Francis, we know, was tremendously impressed by the "poverty" and "littleness" of God—a God who left behind his divine nature, so to speak, and chose to become a vulnerable human child in the womb of the Virgin Mary. In God's entering the human race as a little baby on Christmas Day, Francis saw a God of unbelievable generosity and humility—a God of total self-giving, of smallness and of poverty, who held nothing back from human beings.

The *poverty and smallness of God* made a strong impression on St. Francis, according to evidence in his Rule. In the sixth chapter, Francis instructs his followers that they should "serve the Lord in Poverty...because the Lord *made himself poor* for us in this world." Anthony would have read this rule often. More than this, he would have taken to heart the larger spiritual vision of St. Francis, which extended beyond his fascination with the feast of Christmas.

St. Francis also saw—in Christ's death on the cross—God's poverty and vulnerability and his desire to make himself small out of love for us. Francis also saw God's poverty in the Eucharist, as well, where under the common forms of bread and wine Jesus humbly hands his whole self over to us, making himself small for us on the altar.

To see St. Anthony holding the infant Jesus in his arms, therefore, is to see a true follower of St. Francis. For did not Francis also embrace that same image of God's smallness and humble love?

St. Anthony, Communicator of God's Word

Another meaningful way to interpret the presence of the Christ Child in the arms of St. Anthony is to realize that Anthony was a great preacher of the gospel, a brilliant communicator, as it were, of the Incarnate Word himself.

Very often the infant in Anthony's arms is portrayed as standing on the holy Bible, which Christians consider the Word of God. Can there be a more obvious symbol and clue that the Christ child in Anthony's arms represents the very embodiment of the Incarnate Word? Often, the child stands on the Bible's open pages as if identified with the Word itself.

As we meditate on this image of St. Anthony holding the Divine infant, we see St. Anthony as a model and ideal for each of us. St. Anthony inspires us to go through life clinging to this wonderful figure of the humble, self-emptying Christ, who makes himself small and accompanies us as a servant of our humanity and of the world's healing. We are invited by Christ to do the same. In the prayer below, take time to contemplate the Christ who loves us and, yet, who comes across as a small child and a humble servant.

> Though he was in the form of God, [Christ Jesus] did not regard equality with God as something to be grasped. Rather he emptied himself, taking the form of a slave, coming in human likeness; and found human in appearance, he humbled himself, becoming obedient to death, even death on a cross. Because of this God greatly exalted him and bestowed on him the name that is above every name.... (Philippians 2:6–9, *NAB*)

There are not a great number of sermon passages written by St. Anthony of Padua that provide fruitful or easy food for thought for people like you and me living in the twenty-first century. In many cases the images, examples, and phrases Anthony uses in his preaching are not always easy to apply to our lives today. Yet as a writer who has done considerable research on this great Franciscan saint, I can affirm neverthe-less that solid food for reflection does exist in a good number of Anthony's sermons. And the following sermon passage is a powerful example of this.

> "During the Meal, Jesus took bread, blessed it and broke it as a sign that his body should be broken, too, through his freely accepted death. The humanity of Christ is like the grape because it was crushed in the winepress of the cross so that his blood flowed forth over all the earth.... How great is the charity of the beloved! How great the love of the Bridegroom for his spouse, the Church!"

In this passage, St. Anthony gives us a strong glimpse of the immense love of Christ for each human being, including him-self. It is as if Anthony has experienced within himself the full force of Jesus' words, "No one has greater love than this, to lay down ones life for one's friends" (John 15:13). Christ's love for the people of God, Anthony tells us quite vividly is like the love of a bridegroom for his bride.

May St. Anthony's words help us see with renewed faith what the Eucharist teaches us about God's forgiveness and unconditional love for each of us! If you and I understood as clearly as St. Anthony the depth of God's love for each of us, surely our love for Christ would grow stronger.

The Peace Prayer of St. Francis

Lord, make me an instrument of your peace.
Where there is hatred, let me sow love,
Where there is injury, pardon,
Where there is doubt, faith,
Where there is despair, hope,
Where there is darkness, light,
And where there is sadness, joy.
O Divine Master, grant that I may not so much seek
to be consoled as to console;
to be understood as to understand;
to be loved as to love;
for it is in giving that we receive,
it is in pardoning that we are pardoned ,
and it is in dying that we are born to eternal life.

CHAPTER FOURTEEN

The Peace Prayer of St. Francis

Few prayers are more popular around the world and better loved than the Peace Prayer of St. Francis. Nearly everyone acknowledges a happy marriage between the words of the prayer and the generous, joy-filled, and peace-loving spirit of St. Francis of Assisi.

What may surprise many readers is that St. Francis is not the author of this prayer, which has borne his name for over half a century. No serious scholar today, Franciscan, or otherwise, would place the Peace Prayer among the authentic writings of St. Francis.

In recent decades it has become clear that the prayer originated during the early years of the 1900s, but until recently no one has pinpointed the exact year. Finally, researchers are getting to the bottom of the mystery.

Some time ago, a Franciscan confrere gave me the e-mail address of French scholar Dr. Christian Renoux of the University of Orleans in France, who was on top of the latest research. In 2001, Renoux authored a book in French, entitled *La priere pour la paix attribuee a saint Francois. Une enigme a resoudre (The Peace Prayer Attributed to St. Francis: A Riddle to Be Solved).* It was published in Paris by Les Editions Franciscaines.

Asked if he could summarize his findings, Dr. Renoux kindly agreed to do so. This could well be the first time that some of these details have been published in English, at least to such a wide audience. Here are his findings:

The first appearance of the Peace Prayer occurred in France in 1912 in a small spiritual magazine called *La Clochette* ("the little bell"). It was published in Paris by a Catholic association known as 'La Ligue de la Sainte-Messe' ("The Holy Mass League"), founded in 1901 by a French priest, Father Esther Bouquerel (1855–1923). The prayer bore the title of 'Belle priere a faire pendant la messe' ("A Beautiful Prayer to Say During the Mass") and was published anonymously. The author could possibly have been Father Bouquerel himself, but until now the identity of the author remains a mystery.

The prayer was sent in French to Pope Benedict XV in 1915 by the French Marquis Stanislas de La Rochethulon. This was soon followed by its 1916 appearance, in Italian, in the *Osservatore Romano*. Around 1920, the prayer was printed by a French Franciscan priest on the back of an image of St. Francis with the title 'Priere pour la paix' ("Prayer for Peace") but without being attributed to the saint. Between the two World Wars, the prayer circulated in Europe and was translated in English.

The first translation in English that we know of appeared in 1936 in *Living Courageously*, a book by Kirby Page (1890–1957), a Disciple of Christ minister, social evangelist, writer, and editor of *The World Tomorrow*. Page clearly attributed the text to St. Francis of Assisi. During the Second World War and immediately after, this prayer for peace began circulating widely as the Prayer of St. Francis and over the years has gained a worldwide popularity with people of all faiths.

Reflecting on the Peace Prayer

Though written in simple language, the Peace Prayer is a profound statement and a rich springboard for reflection. What follows are my personal meditations inspired by this famous prayer.

Lord, make me an instrument of your peace.

Like that of Christ, our mission on earth is to bring to others God's peace—God's state of "perfect well-being" and completeness. *Shalom* is the Hebrew word for this rich concept of "peace." Often used as a greeting of peace, *Shalom* is a wish that those so greeted will find healing and fullness of life. St. Francis saw this as his mission, too. In his Rule of 1223, he advised his followers that in going about the world "they do not quarrel or fight with words, or judge others; rather let them be meek, peaceful and unassuming, gentle and humble, speaking courteously to everyone, as is becoming.... *In whatever house* they enter, let them say: *Peace to this house*" (cf. Luke 10:5). Good advice for all of us!

Where there is hatred, let me sow love,

God is a fountain of overflowing and unconditional love. God does not choose to return hate for hate, but only love, forgiveness, and healing. As God affirms through Ezekiel, "I have no pleasure in the death of the wicked, but that the wicked turn from their ways and live" (33:11). When nails of hatred were driven into Jesus' hands and feet, what flowed forth from Jesus' wounds in response was not hatred or violent retaliation, only unconditional and healing love. The five wounds of St. Francis suggest a similar love—one that seeks only the other's true welfare.

Where there is injury, pardon,

During the violence-ridden Crusades, St. Francis discovered a path of peace, pardon, and nonviolence. The little poor man went to Egypt to engage in a peaceful dialogue with the sultan or head of the Muslim forces—a meeting in which a spirit of forgiveness, respect, and understanding prevailed. We recall, too, the famous story of Francis granting pardon to a wolf that was terrorizing an Italian village. St. Francis' creative way of brokering peace between the wolf and the villagers is instructive for us today, who are so quick to see violence as the only remedy against terrorism.

Where there is doubt, faith,

When as a young man Francis found himself in a fog of confusion and doubt, he sought the face of God through prayer in caves and other solitary places. God opened Francis' eyes of faith. One day, the saint suddenly saw a vision of Christ gazing at him from the cross with great love. This experience, which has been mentioned more than once in this book, dispelled the fog of doubt from Francis, and he went through the world setting others free from the burden of doubt.

Where there is despair, hope,
Where there is darkness, light,

Think of loving parents patiently caring for children with severe disabilities. They represent the triumph of hope and human goodness over despair and darkness. Recall how St.

Francis kissed lepers and lovingly washed their sores. Surely, many of these suffering souls felt an inner surge of hope and human dignity when they experienced Francis' care.

And where there is sadness, joy.
The secret of St. Francis' joyful spirit was his vibrant belief in a God of overflowing goodness and love. Behind the mask of reality, Francis did not see a dark void but rather an all-loving Creator who sent his only Son to lead us to fullness of life, no matter what the personal cost.

> *O Divine Master, grant that I may not so much seek*
> *to be consoled as to console;*
> *to be understood as to understand;*
> *to be loved as to love;*
> *for it is in giving that we receive,*
> *it is in pardoning that we are pardoned ,*
> *and it is in dying that we are born to eternal life.*

Francis of Assisi may not have *written* the words of the prayer that has been so often attributed to him, but he certainly *lived* them. Everyone who is able to read and understand these words, moreover, readily sees that they communicate the heart of the Gospels and capture what is most essential in the world's great religions. The Peace Prayer of St. Francis is a deep well of spiritual wisdom. We are wise to visit this well often.

St. Francis and His Spirit of Joy
We have already taken to heart in previous chapters St. Francis' astonishing sense of the overflowing goodness of God. We have recalled, more than once, the time Francis had a vision

of Christ looking at him from the cross with such love that his "soul melted" and we remember, later, his mystical experience of receiving the stigmata on Mount LaVerna, near Assisi.

From then on, Francis would often fall into tears, as if that amazing experience of God's incredible goodness and love were forever branded on his soul. The God Francis experienced was the God who chose to be poor and small, and who poured out everything for the love of humankind and held back absolutely nothing. This caused the little saint to go about weeping and proclaiming that "love is not loved"—that God is madly in love with us and we don't respond in kind. This lavish, unconditional love is the kind of love that Francis saw shining through the Word-made-flesh and through all of God's creation.

At times, according to Francis' biographer, Thomas of Celano, Francis would be walking along and suddenly get carried away with the thought of God's goodness. The saint would pick up two sticks from the ground, tuck one under his chin like a violin and move the other over it like a bow. Then he would sing in French songs of love and praise to God. "This whole ecstasy of joy," Celano writes, "would often end in tears and his song of gladness would be dissolved in compassion for the passion of Christ."[1]

Going About the World as Minstrels
Francis wanted to hear music and song even when he was dying. He asked his brother friars to praise God with him by singing the *Canticle of the Creatures,* which he had composed while he was ill and going blind. He used to say, moreover, that he wanted his friars to go about the world like minstrels to

"inspire the hearts of people and to stir them to spiritual joy."
Some followers of St. Francis are still trying to do this in our
times. In the early 1990s in Cincinnati, one of our Franciscan
friars, Fr. Silas Oleksinski, O.F.M., at age sixty-eight had vol-
unteered to serve in the former Soviet Union, where new foreign missionary opportunities were opening up. At an age
when most people are settling into a life of retirement, this
friar was risking separation from loved ones and facing fears
of the unknown. In the early 1990s at a Franciscan church
in Cincinnati, I attended a farewell ceremony designed
for Franciscan missionaries about to depart for a foreign
assignment.

In the Spirit of Franciscan Joy
In the true spirit of Franciscan exuberance, Silas did an amazing thing near the close of the ceremony, as the choir began
singing "How Great Thou Art." It was one of those creative
Franciscan moments that observers of the Order have almost
come to expect from the friars. Silas walked up to the micro-
phone and began whistling—yes, whistling—with the choir,
with a loud and clear, marvelously warbling whistle—all the
way to the last note! It was an almost literal compliance with
Francis' wish that his followers go through the world like minstrels. Several years ago, Silas passed on to the next life and, no
doubt, is presently whistling joyfully in God's glorious presence.

*St. Francis, show all of us how to be joyful followers of you.
And teach us how to go about the world as minstrels, inspir-
ing the hearts of your people and stirring them to spiritual joy.
Amen.*

A Prayer of St. Clare

Look upon Him who became contemptible for you,
and follow Him, making yourself contemptible in this world
for Him.
O most, noble Queen,
Gaze upon Him,
Contemplate Him,
as you desire to imitate him.
If you suffer with Him, you will reign with him.
If you weep with Him, you shall rejoice with Him;
If you die with Him on the cross of tribulation,
you shall possess heavenly mansions in the splendor of the
saints
and you shall live forever.